12.95

DATE DUE		
DEC 0 3 1996	FEB 2 8 2003	
FEB 1 2 1997		
FEB 1 8 1998		
APR 1 1 1998		
FEB 1 5 1999		
MAR 0 8 2000		
MAR 0 1 2001		
DEC 2 2 2001		
FEB 0 7 2002		
JUL 0 5 2002		

Mardi Gras
in the Country

Mary Alice Fontenot

Mardi
Gras
in the
Country

Illustrated by Patrick Soper

PELICAN PUBLISHING COMPANY
Gretna 1995

*The word "Pelican" and the depiction of a pelican are trademarks
of Pelican Publishing Company, Inc.,
and are registered in the U.S. Patent and Trademark Office.*

Library of Congress Cataloging-in-Publication Data

Fontenot, Mary Alice.
    Mardi Gras in the country / by Mary Alice Fontenot ; illustrated
by Patrick Soper
        p. cm.
        Summary: Marianne and Claude visit their grandmother in southwest
Louisiana for the famous country Mardi Gras.
        ISBN 1-56554-033-6
        [1. Carnival—Fiction. 2. Louisiana—Fiction. 3. Cajuns-
Fiction.] I. Soper, Patrick, ill. II. Title.
    PZ7.F73575Mar 1994
    [Fic]—dc20   93-44341
                                                                           CIP
                                                                            AC

Manufactured in China

Published by Pelican Publishing Company, Inc.
1101 Monroe Street, Gretna, Louisiana 70053

The Mardi Gras come from everywhere
all around the countryside;
they come once a year to ask for a donation,
even a sweet potato or some onions.

TRADITIONAL MARDI GRAS CHANT

MARDI GRAS IN THE COUNTRY

"Wake up, Marianne! It's Mardi Gras!"

It was Maw-Maw Badeaux at the bedroom door, the light from her kerosene lamp casting weird shadows on the cypress-plank floor.

Marianne turned over and sleepily drew the patchwork quilt over her head. Hardly ten seconds later she popped up like a jack-in-the-box.

"Mardi Gras!" she exclaimed. "It's Mardi Gras!"

She smothered a yawn, rubbed her eyes, and pushed her long blonde hair away from her face, forgetting all thoughts of more sleep.

Marianne, ten years old, and her six-year-old brother, Claude, lived in town. Maw-Maw Badeaux lived in the country. This year, for the first time, the band of Mardi Gras riders was scheduled to stop at Maw-Maw Badeaux's farm.

The route of the annual Mardi Gras run was supposed to be a secret, but somehow the word always got around, and the farm people who lived on the designated roadways made their plans to welcome the fun-loving visitors and to be entertained in return.

As soon as Maw-Maw Badeaux had been assured that the Mardi Gras riders would stop at her place, she invited Marianne and Claude to spend the night at the farm and asked the other grandchildren to join them for the day.

So for the first time Marianne and Claude were to experience *le courir du Mardi Gras,* the Mardi Gras run, instead of hearing their elders tell about it.

The Badeaux farm was only three miles from the country store where the costumed and masked riders gathered at daybreak on Shrove Tuesday, the day before the Lenten season began. Maw-Maw had insisted on an early bedtime so that the children could get dressed and eat breakfast before the fun started.

Claude was eating cane syrup and *pain perdu,* the Cajun equivalent of French toast, when Marianne joined him at the kitchen table. Maw-Maw Badeaux, one eye on the lane leading up to the farmhouse, was washing and drying the breakfast pots and pans.

"They're here! Here they are!" Maw-Maw threw down her dish towel and hurried to the side door, Marianne and Claude right behind her.

"Shucks! It's only the cousins!" said Claude.

Tante Elodie and her seven-year-old twin girls, Malise and Elise, came in, breathing vapor from the icy outside air.

"Did you bring some nickels?" Claude asked the girl cousins.

Malise and Elise opened mittened hands to show several five-cent coins, the *cinq sous* begged by the Mardi Gras maskers in return for entertainment.

"I have lots of nickels in my pocket," bragged Claude, proud to show what he knew about Mardi Gras customs.

Maw-Maw's house was constructed like many others in the prairie area of south Louisiana. The front porch, built of sturdy cypress, faced the lane, about a quarter of a mile long, that gave access to the main road. Here the children waited for the Mardi Gras riders. Since by eight o'clock the bright sunshine had taken some of the chill out of the frosty morning, they sat, warmly dressed, on the floor of the porch, their legs dangling over the edge.

The Mardi Gras celebration in the country was different from the parades and grand balls of New Orleans. The country people had their own way of having a final fling at merrymaking before observing the solemn Lenten rules of penance, abstinence, and fasting imposed by the Church.

Marianne and Claude knew all about the country Mardi Gras. Maw-Maw Badeaux had prepared them well. She told how weeks in advance of the day, the country women stitched up gaudy costumes for their men to wear on the run.

The "Mardi Gras," as the riders were called, had to follow some rules, Maw-Maw said. Only the leader and his assistants could ride unmasked; this leader, called *"le capitaine,"* searched each rider for weapons before the ride could begin; no one was allowed to use offensive language; and any damage to property was to be repaired within twenty-four hours.

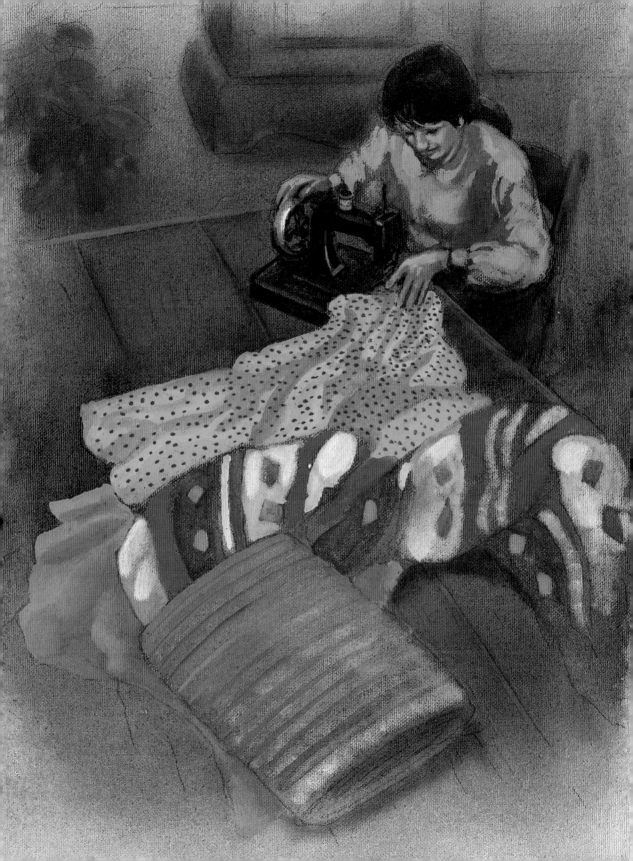

Claude found it hard to sit still and wait. He chattered excitedly with the twins, craning his neck to get a first glimpse of the expected visitors.

Marianne, out on the porch with the younger children, shared their excitement in a quieter way. Her anticipation of fun was mixed with some uneasy feelings. Maw-Maw's stories of the run had included some things that were, as she had put it, "not pretty." Once a rider's *cochonnerie* (crude behavior) had ended up in a fistfight and bitter feuding with an entire family; on another ride a masker, in hot pursuit of a chicken, cut his leg on a barbed-wire fence.

"I see them!" Claude cried, running to the cypress *pieux* (rail) fence that surrounded the house. The other children climbed up beside him. Maw-Maw and Tante Elodie came out on the porch, wiping hands on their calico aprons.

"I'm scared!" said Malise.

17

"Me too!" said Elise. She turned and ran to her mother.

Claude looked a bit fearful, but insisted that he wasn't at all scared. "Malise, you've seen Mardi Gras before," he chided. "Why are you scared?"

"They're so ugly, and they tease children!" Malise replied.

The riders, with their captain in the lead, halted their horses at Maw-Maw's lane. The captain turned his horse to face his men; he seemed to be giving them commands.

"Maw-Maw," said Marianne, "those tall cone-shaped hats they're wearing, are those what you call *capuchons*?"

"Yes," her grandmother answered. "You see, long ago European peasants celebrated Mardi Gras by wearing costumes and masks that made fun of people in power. They wore the *capuchons* to imitate the fine lords and ladies. See that fellow with the square hat like the ones college graduates wear? They wore those to mock the scholars, the learned men."

"Look at those masks!" Marianne exclaimed.

"Oh yes, the women make them," Maw-Maw said. "They use shears to cut the masks from screen wire, then shape them to fit the face. They paint on the eyes and mouth—the uglier the better! Look at that one! His wife made him a long, pointed nose so he'd look even more hideous!"

"Oh, he is ugly!" Marianne said. "Who is he?"

"The whole idea," Maw-Maw continued, "is for no one to know who they are. They do all sorts of things to keep from being recognized—trade costumes with each other, even wear borrowed shoes!"

It was Claude's turn to ask a question. "How long have they been doing this here?"

His aunt elected to answer. "For a long, long time," Tante Elodie said. "My *grand-père* used to tell us stories about running Mardi Gras."

Before Tante Elodie could continue, everyone's attention was drawn away by the sound of a horse's hooves on the lane. The captain had finished giving his men their instructions and was galloping toward the house.

When he reached the fence, he dismounted, tied up his horse, and approached the porch. He wore a purple cloak lined with gold-colored fabric and carried a white flag and a whip made of rope. Claude noticed that a *corne-à-vache*, a cow horn, was slung from the pommel of his saddle.

"Bonjour, Madame Badeaux!" he said, taking off his hat and bowing ceremoniously. *"Tu veux recevoir les Mardi Gras?"* This was the traditional request for permission for the Mardi Gras to come into the yard.

Maw-Maw Badeaux readily agreed to receive the riders. *"Oui, M'sieu le Capitaine!"* she said. "Yes! Come in!"

Without further ceremony the captain blew a loud blast on his cow horn, then invited the waiting riders to enter by waving his flag.

The riders spurred their horses and came thundering down the lane, the horses' hooves stirring up splashes of mud. Bringing up the rear was a buggy carrying the musicians—a masked man playing the accordion, and the driver, also in full costume. As soon as he set down the reins, he picked up his *'tit fer,* his triangle, and prepared to keep time for the accordion player.

The riders dismounted swiftly and tied their horses to the fence alongside the captain's and to the chinaberry trees near the barn. They ran, danced, skipped around, and jumped with abandon, singing and yelling.

"Look at that!" said Tante Elodie, pointing to one of the noisiest and ugliest Mardi Gras. "What a *paillasse!* What a clown!"

This masker appeared bolder than the others. He ran up on the porch and tried to kiss Marianne. She ducked, and he grabbed Maw-Maw Badeaux and swung her around in a Cajun two-step.

Noting what was happening, the captain jumped up on the porch and threatened the Mardi Gras with his whip. The man leaped off the porch and ran around the side of the house.

The children stared open-mouthed at the gaudily dressed men dancing and cavorting around the yard. Several of the maskers linked arms, approached the porch, and sang in squeaky disguised voices, "Give us a fat chicken! Give us a little rice!"

Another Mardi Gras approached the fence with a hand extended, the index finger of the other hand gesturing toward the open palm. His meaning was unmistakable.

"*Cinq sous! Cinq sous!*" he begged in a high-pitched, artificial voice. Like the others, he spoke in Cajun French. Claude and the twins hastily dug out their five-cent coins.

"*Merci, merci!*" The masker bowed low in mock humility and gratitude. Then he tried to kiss Malise's hand, but his screen-wire mask was in the way.

The countryfolk all knew what the masked visitors wanted. They begged for chickens, ducks, guinea hens, and smoked sausage to make gumbo, or for rice to eat with the gumbo, which would be served to the merrymakers and all who came to the dance that night. In return for whatever they were given, the Mardi Gras would entertain with their traditional dancing and singing.

In anticipation of the day, Maw-Maw Badeaux had cooped up two fat chickens. When she figured the children had had enough of the Mardi Gras's foolishness, she went out to the chicken coop, followed by the band of rowdy maskers, who were kept at some distance by the captain and his whip.

Released from the coop, the chickens took off across the field, pursued by the shouting maskers. The children laughed until the tears rolled down their faces.

The Mardi Gras ran in all directions, some chasing the chickens from behind, some trying to run ahead to catch them from the front. They bumped into each other, slid in the mud, and cavorted until finally both chickens were tightly held under the arms of Mardi Gras.

The captain blew his cow horn to assemble the merrymakers. The men untied their horses and mounted, ready to ride again. The fun at the Badeaux farm was over.

The twins ran into the house to join their mother. Claude was still on the top rail of the *pieux* fence, where he had climbed to watch the chicken chase.

All of a sudden the ugly *paillasse* Mardi Gras dashed from the side of the house and grabbed Claude. He threw the kicking and screaming boy over his shoulder and started toward his horse.

Marianne reacted immediately. She ran through the gate, demanding, "Put him down! Put him down!"

The man paid no attention. He got onto his horse, still clutching the yelling Claude.

Marianne grabbed the man's leg and bit it.

"*Yi-yi!* Oh, *yi-yi!*" the man yelled. He loosened his hold on Claude, and the boy slid down to the ground.

"Marianne! Marianne!" the masker said. "Don't you know it's me, your daddy?" He pulled his mask down a few inches.

Marianne felt weak, almost giddy, with relief. This crazy creature was her own father! Claude was laughing; Maw-Maw Badeaux was laughing. The masked merrymakers had gathered around and were enjoying the little trick one of them had played on his children. One held a squawking hen under his arm.

"*Allons à l'autre voisin!*" the captain commanded. "Let's visit another neighbor!" And off they went, chanting the Mardi Gras song.

"Maw-Maw!" exclaimed Marianne. "May we come back next year?"

"Please, Maw-Maw!" echoed Claude.

Maw-Maw smiled, pleased that the grandchildren had been entertained by *le courir.* "Let's go in." She led the way into her warm kitchen.

"Maw-Maw," said Marianne, "what about the dance tonight? Tell us!"

"All right," said Maw-Maw, settling into her rocking chair. Claude stretched out on the kitchen rug, tired out after all the excitement of the morning. Before Maw-Maw could begin, Claude was sound asleep.

Maw-Maw told about the fun and laughter when the masked Mardi Gras dash onto the crowded dance floor, screeching and yelling, playing tricks on the dancers, while the captain pursues them with his whip.

Marianne listened, taking in every word, imagining the scene as Maw-Maw told about it. "And do the Mardi Gras dance with the girls?" she asked.

"Indeed they do," said Maw-Maw. "Just wait a few more years and you'll see for yourself! You know, your father and mother fell in love at a Mardi Gras dance. She had just had her fourteenth birthday, and it was her first dance. He didn't look at another girl after he danced with your mama."

Tante Elodie was waiting her turn to add to the story. "I remember that dance," she said. "I had such a good time! You know, young people in the country do most of their courting at the dances!"

"Then," Maw-Maw continued, "at the stroke of midnight everything comes to an end. The musical instruments are put away, the parents collect their unmarried daughters, and everybody leaves quietly for home. The fun is over, because the forty-day Lenten season has started."

Marianne almost didn't hear the end of Maw-Maw's story. She was daydreaming about an almost-grown-up girl named Marianne out on the dance floor, laughing at the Mardi Gras, dancing and dancing as the music played on and on. . . .